# How to Be a You  Millionaire

## The biggest money-making strategies that you can apply in the next 30 days on YouTube

## by Sean K. Michael

**Check out more Hot information on YouTube @**

www.velocityvideosonline.com

# Table of Contents

# Introduction

Just after a decade since its launch, YouTube has become one of the most successful websites of all time!

Think about this for a second: **could you imagine a world without it?**

With Google's acquisition of YouTube for **$1.65 billion** just a year after its launch in 2005, YouTube has exponentially grown into a multi-billion dollar enterprise that allows anyone to upload valuable user-generated content or corporate media videos.

Steve Chen, Chad Hurley, and Jared Karim, the founders and creators of YouTube, conceptualized the idea of having a platform to share video clips online. During that time, there was no easy way to share videos with friends or relatives unless they was shown to them in person, and so the idea of a video sharing website surfaced.

Little did they know that their idea would evolve into **something so powerful that it would greatly influence many of the aspects of modern society**—from personal expression, media, business, and education to the entertainment industry.

Since it is the most popular video hosting website, many may know YouTube as a great **source for all kinds of entertainment and interesting, up-to-date information about practically any topic under the sun.**

But not everyone knows the true value of YouTube for entrepreneurs, businesses, huge corporations, aspiring artists, or anyone who just wants to showcase and share their hobbies, interests, talents, and expertise with the world.

In short, few people are familiar with the other **advantages or benefits of watching videos or making their own YouTube channel.**

In this book, you will become familiar with maximizing the powerful capabilities of YouTube, especially when it comes to growing your YouTube channel and earning money.

You will also become acquainted with the different marketing strategies and specific action points that you could apply to your own YouTube handle.

**By the time you've finished this book, you will know how to optimize your channel, generate more views and subscribers and enhance your business or products to gain income!**

Enjoy reading!

# CHAPTER 1

# Music Superstars

Whether you're looking for a song to sing in the shower or a playlist at your party, YouTube is definitely one of the best sources for quality music that is current, classic and everything in between.

On YouTube you can search for the latest and most popular music videos and song covers from a variation of genres. Not only does YouTube satisfy your need for great music, it is also a **great platform for famous or up-and-coming musicians to showcase their talent, build their fan base, get signed with a record label, and reach millions of people from all over the planet.**

There are actually numerous celebrities today who were discovered or became famous due to uploading videos on their YouTube channel.

If your dream is to become a famous singer, guitarist, drummer or cover artist, **making a YouTube channel might just be your golden ticket to fame.**

*The figures listed below are according to the YouTube statistics (as of March 2015) that are published on socialblade.com.*

## Boyce Avenue

**YouTube Channel:** https://www.youtube.com/user/boyceavenue

**Videos Uploaded:** 250
**Views:** 1,816,567,283
**Subscribers:** 6,838,733

**Estimated Yearly Earnings: $149.6K - $2.4M**

When you are an aspiring musician on YouTube, you have the chance of becoming more popular than some of the most famous bands and solo artists that we know and love. If you look at the numbers, believe it or not, you see that one particular independent band has more YouTube followers than Linkin Park, Maroon 5, Lady Gaga and even Ariana Grande.

Brothers Alejandro, Fabian, and Daniel Manzano, from Florida, grew up not knowing that they would make a million-dollar career doing what they love most—making great music. The trio decided to form a band back in 2004 and start making music together.

**Boyce Avenue** was officially formed when the older brother, Daniel, moved back to Florida after graduating from Harvard Law School. They decided to name their band by combining the names of the streets that they grew up in.

Fortunately for them and their 6.8 million subscribers, they decided to broaden their audience and upload videos on You-Tube in 2007.

In 2011, they decided to become independent and put up their own recording label(which they named 3 Peace Records.) Boyce Avenue is known for their acoustic covers of their favorite songs and original music. Their first videos that gained a lot of attention were their rendition of Linkin Park's Shadow of the Day, Coldplay's Viva la Vida, and Rihanna's Disturbia.

When the music that they recorded in their garage gained a lot of positive feedback from YouTube viewers, they just knew that they had to make more. The band was even deemed by usatoday.com as **"YouTube's most followed indie band."** In an interview, Alejandro explained that they wanted to expand their reach and get their music to as many people as possible.

They began by uploading at least three videos a month, and they have been doing that ever since. Their fame on YouTube has definitely helped jump-start their careers from making music from their home to touring all over the world.

**One of the most distinguishable characteristics of their channel is that they collaborate with a lot of other singers and artists.** They have done covers with other famous YouTubers and artists like Fifth Harmony, Kina Grannis, Bea Miller, Tyler Ward, Megan Nicole, and many more.

They have gained a lot of attention from millions of people by doing covers of some of the most popular or current songs.

They did this to become more relatable and searchable. By properly utilizing the power of YouTube, the band has performed live in front of massive audiences from the Philippines to Singapore, US, Canada, and Europe and have sold millions of tracks online.

But by 2008, after being on YouTube for a year and receiving a lot of positive feedback from fans and offers from record labels, they knew that their band was on to something and it was going to be big. By the fall of 2008, the trio decided to make music together full time.

When asked about the opportunities that YouTube has brought them that they wouldn't have gotten if they were traditional artists, Fabian said, **"I think the opportunities of YouTube are just that we've had more control. *You can almost create your own opportunities; take your own paths.*"** Alejandro added the fact that YouTube allows anyone to showcase practically anything that they want—**"You have the opportunity to show your fans all those sides of you. That's what I think is kind of the cool part about it."** For instance, anyone from a musician to a comedian to a beauty guru can express his or herself and be his or her own person.

According to Nielsen SoundScan, Boyce Avenue has already sold about 2.5 million tracks and 175, 000 albums. They also have sold-out numerous live shows in Europe, Asia, and played hundreds of thousands of shows around Canada, Australia, the US, Dubai, and elsewhere.

# TIPS FROM BOYCE AVENUE

## 1. Be Committed and Consistent

*"Know yourself, know your sound, commit to it and really just work hard and be consistent."* –Daniel Manzano

When they were just starting out, the Manzano brothers wanted to add flair to what they were doing, so they thought about the things that they could do differently in their channel. But, instead of coming up with an original and unique idea that would make them stand out from the rest of the musicians on YouTube, they chose to do what works for them and stick with their "acoustic vibe".

## 2. Look at the bigger picture

Fabian pointed out the importance of looking at the "whole package holistically". That is, up-and-coming artists or musicians on YouTube must consider the importance of being consistent with their content and branding. A channel that doesn't have a central theme or has a lot of different things going on will not have a significant impact on the viewers, especially in the long term. For instance, if your YouTube thumbnails don't look the same, your viewers will find it rather difficult to identify your channel.

## 3. Know your strengths

*"I think at the end of the day we've all been playing music long enough to where we know our strengths, so it almost doesn't matter if it's an original or a cover."* –Alejandro Manzano

Their years of playing music together as a family as well as their experience with touring all over the world has definitely helped them hone and develop their skills and talent. This has allowed them to really become familiar with each other's strengths, and enabled them to easily find the right instruments, key and arrangements, whenever they work on a video.

## Kurt Hugo Schneider

**YouTube Channel:** https://www.youtube.com/user/KurtHugoSchneider

**Videos Uploaded:** 234
**Views:** 1,116,679,385
**Subscribers:** 5,395,323

**Estimated Yearly Earnings: $90.9K-$1.5M**

If you love listening to music or watching different song covers on YouTube, then you have probably come across Kurt Hugo Schneider's channel.

Aside from being an extraordinary musician, Kurt is also an outstanding student. In high school, he graduated as the class valedictorian and also in 2010 graduated with a degree in mathematics from Yale University, magna cum laude. His career as a musician started when he and Sam Tsui produced both original and cover songs, while they were both still studying. **His breakout video was their medley of Michael Jackson's songs back in 2009.**

**He was then featured on shows like Oprah and Ellen.**
Kurt knew that he wanted to be a musician and write music for
a career when he was finishing college at Yale. During his last
year as a student, his career as a musician on YouTube started
taking off.

Kurt Hugo Schneider is one of the most talented musicians on
YouTube. His 5.3M subscribers are able to enjoy his style of
composing, arranging, and producing various covers of some
of today's most popular songs.

He is not only able to play a variety of instruments, he is also
skilled in filming, directing, and editing his videos. **He is also
famous for collaborating with other YouTube stars
such as Max Schneider, Victoria Justice, Alex Goot,
and Sam Tsui, among others.** When he was just starting
out on YouTube, his only goal was to create and publish videos
that he liked and thought were good.

In an interview, when asked if he had a specific mindset when
he was starting out on YouTube, he said that becoming a
famous musician, filmmaker or producer was just "a dream at
the back of my head."

Like other famous YouTubers, Kurt did not gain a lot of subscribers or attention during his first year of being on YouTube.

**In fact, after one year of creating and publishing vid-
eos online, his total followers only summed to around
3,000.** He only had basics when he was just beginning to
create original content on YouTube. He only had an electric

keyboard, regular recording equipment, and simple editing software. The ability to start small is the main reason why more and more independent artists have the opportunity to be on YouTube.

They need only the basic instruments and computer programs to begin. The low-cost startup expenses allow for affordability."...it's very attainable for the average person to produce great stuff now, which is why there is good stuff on YouTube. You don't need to be paying a ton of money an hour for a studio and thousands and thousands for every single time you want to shoot anything."

## LESSONS FROM KURT HUGO SCHNEIDER

### 1. Find interesting ways of showing things

Kurt believes that a lot of musicians on YouTube overlook the visual aspect of their videos. He says that, unlike other platforms for music, such as Spotify or iTunes, people go on YouTube not just for the music per se, but also for the visuals—*"People go on YouTube because they want to see it, so no matter whether you're a musician or whatever you're doing online, the visuals trump all else, so you gotta focus on the visuals and find interesting ways of showing things."*

### 2. In doing covers, do it your way

In making song covers, Kurt makes sure that he adds his own flair to each of them. He has no desire to make it sound and look exactly as the original. By putting his own signature to the song, it allows him to come up with various interesting renderings. He and Sam love creating versions of songs that are entirely different from the original.

## 3. Do not give up

Kurt started out by making short clips on YouTube while he was still in college. It was not until his arrangement of Michael Jackson's hits that people really started noticing his work— *"The most important thing is not to give up, because the chance you will post one video and it will go viral is really low."*

## 4. Do what you love

In making videos, you have to make it a priority to only show-case the things that arouse your interest and passion. Doing something that you love will allow you to continue and perse-vere until you experience a breakthrough.

## 5. Be as nice and genuine as you can

When you read about the interviews of YouTubers that Kurt has worked with in the past, you see that he is deemed as one of the kindest and most professional musicians on YouTube. He is able to objectively criticize other singers and instru-mentalists as well as accept the opinions of others. Since he started his career as a YouTuber with his childhood friend Sam Tsui, collaborating with other musicians has not been a problem for him.

# CHAPTER 2

# Quality Food over Quantity

Nowadays, people can become experts just by doing a lot of research online and watching tutorials on YouTube and applying them. Anyone can become a self-taught artist, guitarist, chef, or baker.

## Rosanna Pansino

**YouTube Channel:** https://www.youtube.com/user/RosannaPansino

**Videos:** 265
**Views:** 680,680,509
**Subscribers:** 3,625,727

**Estimated Yearly Earnings: $132.7K - $2.1M**

Before her fame on YouTube, Rosanna Pansino had a fervent desire to land a job in the entertainment industry. She moved to Los Angeles, California, to try to make it in the Hollywood spotlight.

She started out by doing hand commercials and cameos in different shows. In an interview, Rosanna, or Ro (as her followers call her), said that she was encouraged by a friend to start her own YouTube channel for her to be able to practice speaking and be more comfortable in front of a camera.

*"I got tired of waiting for people to give me opportunities, so I started to make them for myself. I used to do a lot of oddball jobs in Hollywood. I was a stand-in. I was a hand double. I had a regular background part on Glee. I booked a few legit acting roles on television shows. And I did some principal roles in commercials. But I'm a really creative person, and I was just kind of tired of waiting for someone to say, 'Okay, you can create things now.'"* (Source: *Interview with seattlemet.com*)

Her very first video was a vlog that featured her and her sister volunteering for Earth Day. **The first equipment that she used was a flip camera worth $80.** She did not start off baking goodies in her channel. She tried and experimented with different video formats, styles and concepts, to see which would best catch her audience's attention.

But, it wasn't until she decided to film and upload a video of her preparing some themed treats that her followers started requesting more videos.

Her love for baking (influenced by her grandmother) caused her to make a DIY (Do-It-Yourself), tutorial type of YouTube channel. She also loves playing video games so she decided to bake the things that were considered nerdy while she was growing up, but now they've become mainstream.

**She makes cakes and pastries that are based on video games, comic books, sci-fi, and fantasy.** She wanted an outlet for her creativity so she decided to showcase her love for baking, gaming, and science fiction in her channel.

Her first baking tutorial video garnered 60,000 views in 30 days. By 2012, Rosanna decided to produce more videos with the same content, thus "Nerdy Nummies" was born.

**Her channel then gradually evolved into "Nerdy Nummies", a series that features her baking geek-themed cupcakes, cakes, and pastries.** The unique combination of gaming and baking is her true break out hit. She now has 3.6m subscribers and a total of 680,680,509 views.

## LESSONS FROM ROSANNA PANSINO

### 1. Quality over Quantity

Her quirky personality and passion for baking are definitely some of the key ingredients that contributed to her success on YouTube. Her ability to stay true to her character and produce original content consistently has attracted millions of viewers all over the world.

Rosanna does not focus on whether her videos will become successful or viral, but instead focuses on creating fun and high quality content for her viewers. Furthermore, Ro believes that her videos are not viral but instead accumulate a lot of views over time. She feels that the success of her videos or channel is gradual and not instant.

## 2. Draw ideas and inspiration from everywhere

Rosanna gets the inspiration for her videos from practically everywhere. She usually features the things that she is excited or happy about; these could come from movies she's watched, comic books she's read, or games she has played.

She values the opinion of her audience, which is why she entertains a lot of requests from her viewers or followers. In fact, she even encourages them to suggest topics or ideas as to how they want her next video to be.

## 3. Develop a procedure and stick to it

The typical process of making one Nerdy Nummies episode usually involves the brainstorming of ideas, purchasing of ingredients, experimenting with recipes, filming, editing, and, finally, uploading the video online.

Rosanna says that the process takes at least five days to complete. The success of her channel could be attributed to the fact that she was able to come up with a successful niche and stay consistent to the kind and quality of videos that she produces.

*"As time went on, my filming schedule became more consistent, and it made sense to hire some help and upgrade my equipment. Once I got into it I realized that I had full creative control of my content and could let my imaginative side out."*

## 4. Share content that you enjoy

When you work on your own YouTube channel, it is important to create videos that are important to you and not just your viewers. Rosanna's success could be credited to the fact that she really enjoyed what she was doing and she had full control over everything that was going on her channel.

*"I've never thought about how to make a video go viral. From the very beginning I have always wanted to use YouTube to better myself and share things I enjoy with the world. If others want to join me on that journey I am happy to have them as viewers."*

## 5. Be Passionate

Rosanna started filming her videos with an $80 flip camera. When she was asked for advice for up and coming YouTubers, she pointed out that, even if you are just starting to learn about filming or editing videos, as long as you are passionate with what you are doing, people will take notice.

*"Even if your equipment isn't the best or you're not the best editor, if you're passionate about it, I think that viewers will see that and respond to that."*

What started off as a small project for her to be more confident and natural in front of the camera evolved into a million-dollar endeavor. After establishing a reputation on YouTube, in 2015, she was offered a partnership with Wilton Enterprises, one of the biggest cake decorating companies in the world. This meant that for the rest of 2015, her videos would be comprised of branded baking tutorials.

# CHAPTER 3

# Unboxing and Toy Stars

From unwrapping toys to making millions—who would have thought that a person, young or old, could make some serious cash by unboxing toys and playing with them?

With the **rise of YouTube's toy unboxing genre**, majority of the toy brand marketers are now knocking on the doors of some of the most subscribed and viewed channels, to have their products featured and reviewed. Some of the most popular channels that unbox and review toys include DisneyCollectorBR, DisneyCarToys, and EvanTubeHD.

## EvanTubeHD

**YouTube Channel:** https://www.youtube.com/user/EvanTubeHD

**Videos Uploaded:** 426
**Views:** 1,161,847,339
**Subscribers:** 1,289,329

**Estimated Yearly Earnings:** $181.5K - $2.9M

EvanTubeHD is a family-friendly toy and game reviewing channel that features 8-year-old Evan and occasionally his mother and sister Jillian. Evan unboxes and reviews a lot of different toys from Angry Birds, and LEGO, to Leap Frog, Spy Gear and everything in between.

Children are more likely to trust the opinion of other kids their age when it comes to choosing their next favorite toy. This may be one of the reasons why EvanTubeHD became such a huge success.

What started out as a way for their family to bond and spend time together has progressed into a million-dollar venture— Jared, Evan's father, decided to start a small father-son project back in 2011.

The first video that they did was an Angry Birds plush toys stop-motion video that was published on September 20, 2011. They never would have thought that they would be on to something big until their video reached 1 million views.

It was on the following month of their YouTube debut that 5-year-old Evan was filmed by his father while talking about their Angry Birds clay figures. After some time, their viewers started requesting more videos of Evan talking about toys, and the rest is history.

With Jared's background in film and photography and Evan's wit, charm, and credibility, **their channel became one of the most sought after toy and game reviewing channels on YouTube.** EvanTubeHD now has over 1 billion views in total and 1.2 million subscribers. According to Jared, they have appointed a sales team to negotiate, sell ads and deal with the different sponsorship offers, toy brands, and companies.

What makes EvanTubeHD unique is that they have developed a strategy wherein their videos are both fun and informative for kids of all ages. They don't just unwrap a specific toy and describe or talk about how they are used.

Instead, Evan, and occasionally his sister and mother, actually **demonstrates how fun and exciting the toys really are.** Evan's appeal, reliability, and humor, coupled with his dad's filming and editing skills, became the perfect recipe for their channel's success.

After three and a half years of being on YouTube, Evan now has three YouTube handles—namely EvanTubeHD where he reviews toys with his sister, EvanTubeRAW, which is comprised of behind the scenes footage of their family life, and EvanTubeGaming where he reviews video games.

Since their channel has significantly grown in popularity over time, Evan's parents opted not to provide personal or identifying information such as their surname to protect their kids. "*My wife and I are a bit hesitant about publishing anything that could be used to track where we live or where the kids go to school,*" says Jared, in an interview published on newsweek.com. As much as possible, they want Evan and his sister to live a normal life like other children.

In an article published on thepennyhoarder.com, Jared sayd he believes that they have built and sustained their presence in the virtual world of YouTube because they are working as a family— *"We work as a tight family unit. Everyone contributes and has their special roles... Family is the driving factor behind everything we do on YouTube."*

## THE IMPACT OF EVANTUBEHD

EvanTubeHD had the upper hand when it comes to uploading high quality videos. This is because Evan's father runs a film and photography business that made it easy for them to make and upload videos on YouTube.

EvanTubeHD and the other YouTube toy unboxing channels have significantly changed the way advertisers or marketers of some of the world's top toy brand companies reach their target audience. The influence of EvanTubeHD as well as the other channels similar to it has opened a new way for businesses to advertise their products.

## LESSONS LEARNED FROM EVANTUBEHD

EvanTubeHD is just one of the plethora of YouTubers that have been making a living out of unboxing toys and other sponsored products. If you want to follow the footsteps of one of the most successful toy reviewing channels on YouTube, here are some of the strategies that we can learn from EvanTubeHD:

## 1. Experiment with new video styles

Since their YouTube debut on 2011, Evan and his family have been uploading consistent content with the same style and set-up; their video always involves Evan sitting behind a table as he plays and reviews toys. But they have recently tried a new filming style wherein Evan together with his whole family roamed and shopped around Toys 'R' Us in search of the perfect gift for Evan's friend. They tried this approach to fully embrace the sponsorship that they have with the aforementioned retail store. They not only made the best out of their sponsorship deal but they also offered their fans something new to look out for.

## 2. Be Authentic

The most important thing that YouTube viewers look for is authenticity. A lot of the famous YouTubers are very cautious when it comes to bringing in sponsors or product placements in their videos. They see to it that they don't appear like a "sell out" whenever they make a sponsored video and EvanTubeHD has been very successful when it comes to being authentic. His expression of joy and wonder whenever he unwraps a new toy is one of the factors that makes his viewers watch more of his videos.

# CHAPTER 4

# Funniest YouTube Sensations

## NigaHiga

**YouTube Channel:** https://www.youtube.com/user/nigahiga Videos Uploaded: 226

**Views:** 2,127,676,686
**Subscribers:** 14,051,388

**Estimated Yearly Earnings: $114.1 K - $1.8M**

Ryan Higa, also known as NigaHiga, has been doing YouTube videos for almost nine years. He is famous for his comedy skits featuring his rants about the most random things, as well as his Dear Ryan segments wherein he reads his followers' comments and suggestions about what they want his next video to be about. **Ryan is one of the first YouTube users whose videos caught the attention of millions of people.**

In many of his interviews, Ryan describes his success on You-Tube as accidental because he only uploaded videos way back in 2006 because it was the easiest way to share videos with his family and friends. He even thought that YouTube was a way to share content with his relatives privately.

His main objective back then was just to have fun and share hilarious skits with the people on YouTube. His channel originally featured a lot funny of lip synching videos of him and his friends. But, unfortunately, when YouTube started to reach more people, his hilarious lip synching videos were removed due to alleged copyright violations.

When those videos were removed from YouTube, Ryan lost over 100 million views. But he did not let that unfortunate incident keep him from uploading more videos on YouTube. From then on, he became very careful with the brands or products that show up in his videos, as well as the music he uses. Now, Ryan is able to produce not only comedy sketches but also original songs and music videos. In 2014, he uploaded music videos such as "Coffee Shop Love" and "S.W.G." in collaboration with Golden, another YouTuber.

In 2012, he and his team of friends started RHPC or Ryan Higa Production Company. Apart from his main channel, Nigahiga, he now has HigaTV, which features other segments such as TEEHEE time where he opens, reads, and plays with fan mail sent by his subscribers from all over the world.

In an interview on CNN, Ryan was asked if he ever felt pressured to come up with original material to stand out among the other famous YouTubers. He answered: "***...not necessarily, there's definitely a lot of other people, but I don't think that because someone is a fan of someone else, they can't be a fan of you. So, the thing is, it is more important to stick to your own voice and not try and follow other voices, or copy what other people are doing.***"

Ryan Higa was able to maintain his YouTube channel throughout the years because he is passionate and focused on what he loves doing. He gave up college to focus on his YouTube channel, with no assurance as to whether he could make a living out of it. He chose to do so because, according to him, college would always be there, but his opportunities with YouTube might just come once in a lifetime.

## ADVICE FROM RYAN HIGA

Similar to the other profiles that are featured in this book, Ryan Higa also believes that in growing your brand or YouTube handle, consistency is key. He even says in an interview that *"the main thing is that you post videos that people want to see; majority of the time, it's comedy. Once you find your own style that works for you, you must continuously produce and post videos."*

### 1. You are your best critic

Before Ryan uploads his new video for the week, he watches it first and thinks of himself as the audience. He double checks to see if his audience will enjoy his new upload and that it doesn't contain any material that could potentially offend them. If it passes his standards, it's ready to be posted.

## 2. Surprise your audience with different video types

In an interview, Ryan shared that he often changes the type of video that he uploads every week. This is his technique to keep his audience engaged because they never know what he will upload next. The types of his videos range from rants and skits to music videos, short films, or spoofs.

## 3. Strive to be better

When asked about his ultimate goal, Ryan said that he wants to continuously produce videos that will exceed or be better than the previous ones he's posted—*"with every new video, I'm trying to improve, whether it's like the video quality, editing, or even the material. I think if you were to look back at the first videos I made, you'd hopefully see that they went from "horrible" to "a little less horrible..." I'll never stop setting new goals and working toward creating the perfect video."*

## 4. Do not be easily discouraged

The internet is filled with people who give a lot of unsolicited advice and even hateful comments. There are people who spam your comments section or even criticize your personal life. You have to understand that the internet is a place where everybody wants to share their opinion. If you want to put yourself out there and be a public image, you cannot let their opinions get to you. The comments section is a great way to connect with your audience and build a relationship with them; but you must remember never to "feed the trolls". Ignore those who do not have anything good or sensible to say.

# Jenna Marbles

**YouTube Channel:** https://www.youtube.com/user/JennaMarbles

**Videos Uploaded:** 246
**Views:** 1,747,292,980
**Subscribers:** 15,018,802

**Estimated Yearly Earnings: $67.3K-$1.1M**

Jenna Mourey, more commonly known as Jenna Marbles, graduated with a degree in psychology and a Master of Education in Sport Psychology and Counseling. Despite her degrees, she still wasn't sure about what she really wanted to do. She had a variety of different full-time jobs that were not related to education.

**Before her fame on YouTube, she was a sports blogger by day and a go-go dancer at night.** It was not until her "How to Trick People Into Thinking You're Good Looking" video that she found her passion for making videos that made people laugh.

She always knew that she wanted to make people laugh and feel happy but she never thought that it would turn out to be her career. Jenna's turning point as a YouTuber began when her self-deprecating video became viral in just a matter of days. Elitedaily.com outlined the main reasons why Jenna Marbles' success skyrocketed despite her being similar to other comedians on YouTube.

# PROBABLE REASONS FOR THE FAME OF JENNA MARBLES

## 1. She speaks her mind

The thing that her fans love the most about her is that she honestly voices her opinions about the most mundane or trivial things. She doesn't filter her language and her fans love her for that.

Both her humor and profanity are what make her stand out from the rest of the comedians on YouTube. Her blunt way of explaining things actually makes real sense. **Basically, she is not afraid to say the things that most people are afraid of saying.**

## 2. She values her experiences

*"In order to find out who you are, you will, at some point, have to feel really isolated, left out, different."*

Jenna published her very own Draw My Life video in 2013 wherein she narrated her life before fame. She talked about the struggles and heartaches she felt as a child.

As a college undergrad she just wanted to know her place in the world. Jenna emphasizes the importance of finding yourself and accepting you for who you are—flaws included. She believes it's okay to be different because that is what makes each and every one of us special and unique in our own way.

### 3. She reminds her fans to take it easy

Although Jenna's videos might involve her ranting about how awful things are happening in her life, she still encourages her viewers not to get too carried away by all the stress of living and to learn to take it easy. She has her own way of reminding her fan base that no matter how hard life gets, it is still better to laugh, move on, and keep moving forward.

## LESSONS YOU'LL LEARN FROM JENNA

### 1. She expresses her own brand of comedy

When you decide to watch one of her videos, you will get used to her impersonating celebrities or ranting about the usual issues that young adults experience today.

She is one of the few YouTubers who is not afraid to go beyond the norm and try out her ideas for her videos regardless of how insane or "painful" they may be. An example is her Kylie Jenner Lip Tutorial wherein she literally put the most random things on her face such as kitty litter, Jalapeno seeds, cinnamon, glue stick and even chalk!

### 2. She values consistency

Since her breakout video on YouTube, Jenna has maintained her style and format of creating and producing videos. Unlike other YouTubers, she did not immediately update her equipment but instead kept her low-cost production paraphernalia. She regularly uploads new videos every Wednesday.

### 3. She does great impersonations

Jenna has mastered the skill of entertaining people without seeming to try too hard. She is great at impersonating celebrities such as Justin Bieber, Snooki, Sarah Palin, and even Lady Gaga. She incorporates these characters into her skits and her fans love her for that. Her own style of comedic blogging has definitely helped her gain hundreds of thousands of views each day even without uploading new content.

### 4. She maximizes her creative freedom

Unlike the usual mainstream comedians, Jenna is not bounded by anything, especially when it comes to her creative freedom. She is able to act, say, and do whatever she wants and she values what her fans want to see. She usually asks her audience for ideas on her next videos.

### 5. She is passionate about her job as a YouTube personality

Most people would assume that a person's rise to fame on any platform would cause him or her to immediately transition into the mainstream media. However, contrary to what most people would think, Jenna has no intention of going mainstream anytime soon—*"I'm not completely sold that you ever have to transition to mainstream media, you know? What I get to do is have fun in my house, by myself, and put it on the Internet"* she revealed in an interview with nytimes.com.

### 6. Advice for up and coming YouTubers

When asked about the secret to online success, Jenna told news.nationalpsot.com that *"Literally anyone can do it. It's*

*just a matter of being honest and coming from a place that's
real and genuine—interacting with people and being open.
Oh, and having thick skin."*

---

## SMOSH

**YouTube Channel:** https://www.youtube.com/user/
smosh

**Videos Uploaded:** 488
**Views:** 4,308,276,875
**Subscribers:** 20,322,380

**Estimated Yearly Earnings: $262.9K-$4.2M**

---

Smosh is one of the few YouTubers who have gained fame on
YouTube since its early years. **The channel of the power-
house duo Anthony Padilla and Ian Hecox is more
popular than that of the mainstream celebrities** such
as Jennifer Lawrence and even Katy Perry.

**A lot of the older generations may not have heard of
SMOSH or may not even have an idea as to who they
really are. But, for their younger counterparts, avid
online viewers might even regard Smosh as the kings
of YouTube. This is because they are one of the longest running YouTube sensations since 2005. One viral
video after another has caused Smosh to run and
handle multiple YouTube channels that are all very
successful.**

**Below is a list of the different SMOSH YouTube channels that you might want to check out:**

- https://www.youtube.com/user/SmoshGames
- https://www.youtube.com/user/ShutUpCartoons
- https://www.youtube.com/user/ShutUpCartoons
- https://www.youtube.com/user/ElSmosh
- https://www.youtube.com/user/TheFrenchSmosh

In an interview, the duo confessed that they were already making videos even before they knew about YouTube. Unlike most budding YouTubers today, Anthony and Ian did not create their very own YouTube channel to gain popularity or fame; they did it as a hobby.

During their first years as YouTubers, no one would have predicted that YouTube would eventually become a substitute or even an alternate medium for entertainment. Now kids spend more time on their laptops, tablets, or smart phones while watching YouTube videos than watching TV. More so, the most famous YouTube stars are even regarded by some blogs and websites as becoming more popular than up-and-coming Hollywood celebrities.

Forbes.com even called the team of Ian and Anthony the "New, Purely Digital, Breed Of Celebrity."

**The duo's first video consisted of them lip-synching to the theme song of Pokemon.** It was actually their breakout video that caused them to gain a lot of traction, not only to their YouTube channel but also to their already established website.

Unfortunately, after getting millions of views, their very first video was removed due to copyright claims. Fortunately, the popularity of Smosh was already apparent in the virtual world when this incident occurred.

Since their parody of the famous Pokemon theme song, Smosh has significantly grown into a multi-million success. Their career skyrocketed even more when they met the former president of Disney's Television Animation, Barry Blumberg, who encouraged and helped them drastically monetize their channel and website.

Because of this, Smosh became one of the first YouTube channels to earn some serious cash. Before YouTube, the most traffic their website got was only around 30,000. When Ian and Anthony partnered with Barry, they were able to focus on their creativity and material while Barry dealt with building their brand and signing deals. **Today Smosh has millions of viewers throughout the world** who know and love their channels. Together they have become digital media moguls.

## LESSONS FROM SMOSH

### 1. Commitment and Devotion

You might think that after a couple of years of uploading videos on YouTube, personalities such as Smosh would find it difficult to sustain creating funny and original material. But after a decade, the duo's fame and success is just getting bigger and bigger.

They have continued to produce top-notch videos. This is because the team they started and the employees hired are dedicated and passionate about what they do.

## 2. Know your audience

Another factor that contributed to the success of Smosh is that they know exactly how to create original content for their viewers. Most of their fan base consists of teens or tweens under the age of 18.

Despite having multiple YouTube handles, Smosh never floods their channels. They only update a few of these channels per week.

The main reason for multiple channels is for them to effectively separate their vlogs or skits from their gaming videos. If you are just starting out on YouTube, you could just focus on building a single channel first and then eventually decide if you want to create another one in the future.

## 3. Expand your passion for business

Smosh is the perfect example of YouTube success because they have successfully expanded their brand outside of the multi-billion video sharing website by making their very own site (smosh.com) as their main platform.

Their company has **gained numerous awards and recognitions throughout the years including the prestigious YouTube Award and Shorty Award.** To say that Smosh has reached the peak of becoming a YouTube sensation is quite an understatement.

They are on the brink of releasing their own feature-length film later this year. Lionsgate has announced that Smosh is going to be releasing their very own movie entitled *Smosh: The Movie* on July 23, 2015.

# CHAPTER 5

# Beautiful YouTubers

When you think back and imagine how the Internet or social media sites were back in 2007, you would be amazed as to how the digital age could completely transform and drastically improve in just under a decade.

Back then, YouTube was only about two years old and the number one social media site was MySpace. During that time, if a person told another that he could make a substantial amount of money just by uploading videos, he or she would probably be thought of as absurd or even crazy.

## Michelle Phan

**YouTube Channel:** https://www.youtube.com/user/MichellePhan

**Videos Uploaded:** 362
**Views:** 1,096,763,671
**Subscribers:** 7,590,837

**Estimated Yearly Earnings: $41.7K - $666.9K**

Can you believe that YouTube sensation, make-up guru, author and successful beauty entrepreneur Michelle Phan was denied a job at a beauty counter?

Michelle was working as a waitress when she decided to apply for a job selling beauty products. She was not given the job because she lacked experience in sales.

Michelle has always been a make-up and beauty enthusiast. So, instead of giving up, she opened her laptop and filmed and uploaded her very first make-up tutorial on YouTube back in 2007.

Her intention was just to share and talk about how she applies her make-up, not knowing that people would actually be interested in it. But, to her surprise, her video garnered over 40,000 views in the span of just one week.

In her Draw My Life video, published on her YouTube channel, Michelle shared the difficulties that she and her family experienced when she was young. They had to move a lot because of her biological father's gambling problem.

She did not have any friends because there were few Asian children in her school. Because of this, she'd spend a lot of time in her room and find comfort and solace in doing art. One of the creations that she drew was a picture of her with superpowers that had the ability to save her family from their situation.

At 17, she worked as a waitress to help to provide for her family. With her mom's help, she was able to enroll in the Ringling College of Art and Design.

Fortunately for Michelle and her millions of followers, in her first semester as a college freshman, she got her hands on her very first laptop that her professors handed out to each student in class.

That particular laptop was used to film her first make-up tutorial, which simply told how she put on cat eyeliner and nude lipstick. **With so much positive feedback and requests from the YouTube community, Michelle kept making videos.** Eventually she earned enough money from ad revenues to allow her to quit her job as a waitress and create YouTube videos full time.

The first make-up brand that approached Michelle was Lancôme. Lancôme Cosmetics made their official YouTube channel in 2009 wherein they spent a lot of money in producing their videos. They hired the best make-up artists and models for their tutorials. To their dismay, despite their delivery of high quality content, their video only got about 500 views.

Puzzled by this finding, an executive from Lancôme wanted to find out why people were more interested in watching make-up tutorials made by girls in their bedrooms than their high-quality videos. Lancôme was able to reach out to Michelle when that same executive typed in "Lancôme Make-up" on YouTube and Michelle's video with half a million views popped up.

This was because Michelle typed in the products that she used for that video as a tag and a Lancôme product happened to be one of them.

In 2010, Michelle became the online spokesperson for Lancôme. In 2011, after four years of making videos with hundreds of thousands and even millions of views each, Google offered Michelle a million dollar deal to make 20 hours of content.

**Michelle's career skyrocketed from being a YouTube make-up guru to building an empire by launching her own make-up brand with L'Oréal,** writing her own book, and becoming one of the most inspirational people on and off the Internet.

## LESSONS FROM MICHELLE PHAN

In an article published on forbes.com Michelle Phan provided a step-by- step strategy to achieve success. According to Michelle, for anyone to become successful, he or she must perceive life as *"the ultimate road trip."*

### Step 1. Know your vision

Before anything else, it is important to at least have an idea of which path you want to pursue. You have to know what you want, or what you want to achieve for you to be able to develop a clear vision of what you want to do with your life. When she began uploading videos on her channel back in 2007, her vision was to "inspire women and build confidence," which she continues to do today but on a much larger or global scale.

### Step 2. Find the right vehicle

*"Pick a car, whether it's a Prius or Mercedes, but you have to make a commitment."*

This piece of advice is applicable to those who want to establish their identity on the online world. Michelle suggests that people who want to make a living out of the Internet should focus on one or two social media networks rather than trying hard to pursue and handle multiple accounts on platforms such as YouTube, Twitter or Facebook.

She says that it is important to prioritize which platforms you're going to concentrate on. For Michelle, despite her multi-million dollar make-up brand (Em Cosmetics), published book, and a partnership with a global multi-platform entertainment company (Endemol), she still independently runs her YouTube channel.

## Step 3. Identify potential co-pilots

For Michelle, her co-pilot is her fan base. She values their comments and suggestions, which significantly helped her career to move in the right direction all these years. Also, Michelle's fan base is mainly comprised of female subscribers but when she collaborated with her fellow YouTuber and video gamer Freddie Wong, her male subscribers grew in numbers.

## Step 4. Optimize your fuel

Michelle also pointed out the importance of knowing what motivates you the most. It is essential to constantly check to see if you are still on the right path towards achieving your goals.

*"You have to have a reason why you're doing something, if you're starting a start-up, if you're*

*developing an app, if you are launching a YouTube channel, you have to ask 'why are you doing this?' 'cause if you don't have a reason why, that's like building a house on top of sand, it's just going to sink. You have to have a strong foundation because that's the motivation that's going to keep fueling you every morning, when you wake up, and to go in and attack. Because if you don't have that foundation, within a year or two, you're going to burn out..."* (source: Re/code interview published on youtube.com)

## Step 5: Scan the road

"Scanning the road" means being sensitive and on top of current trends or styles. She says that it is important not only to look at what's ahead of you but to also be mindful of potential speed bumps or road problems along the way.

## INSPIRATIONAL MESSAGES FROM MICHELLE

In an interview with Re/code, Michelle Phan shared a lot of inspirational messages and advice for aspiring YouTubers or beauty entrepreneurs.

Michelle advises people who want to earn a significant amount of money on YouTube to treat it like any other media or medium of entertainment: *"It's like television or magazines, you have the subscription, but that's not going to make all the money. You need to bring on sponsors, partners, and you also have to sell products especially if you want to grow your brand... I tell all my friends who want to go on YouTube, 'You don't have to have millions of subscribers to be considered successful.' With sponsorships, and viewerships, my friends make around five to six thousand dollars a month, which is not bad especially if you are doing what you love most... You could just roll out of bed, get your laptop, and make a living."*

With her rise to fame and her exponentially growing financial success, Michelle has stayed true to her vision when she first started uploading videos. She loves what she's doing all the more because she is able to provide employment for a great number of people. *"It's not about making money, it's about making the money that could help other people make money,"* she says.

She and three other individuals started a start-up company called Ipsy in 2011, which is a beauty products subscription service that offers its customers glam bags with beauty products that are tailored to their needs.

Their company has grown into a multi-million dollar enterprise that has provided hundreds of jobs to people. ***"The Internet has changed the way people work. Which I think is really exciting because now, this gives us the opportunity as entrepreneurs to create more jobs for people."***

She also underscores the importance of knowing how to do everything yourself:

*"If you've never edited a video, this is going to be tough, I'm going to have to teach you how to do it because you need to learn everything yourself,*

*because that is what makes you different than talent... If you want to be an entrepreneur, you have to learn how to do everything 'cause when you're launching your own business, you're your own lawyer, own PR person ... it's not easy, but it's so rewarding knowing that you were able to do all of that."*

Michelle calls herself a "predator" because she's her own producer, director and editor. She still does her YouTube videos alone and has decided not to hire a production team because she still wants to stay personal and keep in touch with her YouTube fanbase that significantly helped her to get where she is today.

## Bethany Mota

**YouTube Channel:** https://www.youtube.com/user/Macbarbie07

**Videos Uploaded:** 411
**Views:** 691,956,282
**Subscribers:** 8,630,326

**Estimated Yearly Earnings: $39.4K-$630.9K**

Thirteen-year-old Bethany Mota back in 2009 never predicted that she would become such a role model and inspiration to millions of girls from all over the world.

She created her channel on YouTube named Macbarbie07 because she wanted to share make-up and fashion tips with whoever came across her channel.

Little did she know that, just a few years after creating her very first video, **she would become an online star and that would enable her to participate in shows like Dancing with the Stars and even become a guest judge on Project Runway**. Not only has she appeared on numerous shows on national TV but, more than that, she was able to launch her very own clothing line.

Bethany was initially home schooled and did not enter the public school education system until third grade. She was even cyberbullied in 2009, but luckily she found a productive outlet to distract her from all the negativity. She discovered her unexpected hobby: making creative YouTube videos. Fortunately for her millions of fans and subscribers, her outlet was making, shooting, and editing fun and helpful videos all by herself.

When Bethany was just starting out, her videos were mostly comprised of haul videos in which she would showcase the clothing that she just bought.

She is known for uploading creative beauty, fashion and hair and make-up tutorials on her channel. **She is one of the youngest YouTube stars and was even deemed by *Time Magazine* to be one of the 25 most influential teens of 2014.**

Her career as a beauty and fashion guru has grown so large throughout the years that her fan base has already created a name for her followers. They call themselves the "Mota-vators".

Bethany's success has indeed become an inspiration to a lot of young girls and teenagers from across the globe. She has become a role model to them because she shares her experiences and valuable lessons that she has learned throughout her young life.

Her goal as an up-and-coming YouTuber back in 2009 mainly revolved around her wanting to share her passions and interests with her audience.

She made sure to establish a direct line of communication with her fan base. **She is favored by millions of her viewers because of her ability to resonate and relate with them genuinely and effectively.**

She has also experimented with various styles and formats of producing her videos throughout the years to always be up to date and current with the trends.

It was not until she realized that coming up with videos that are in tune with the current trends that her channel really started gaining a lot of views and subscriptions.

Her tutorial on Selena Gomez made her aware of the importance of staying on top of trends. By remaining relevant, she has developed a rapport with her fan base.

Like other YouTube stars, since her unexpected fame in 2009, Bethany Mota's fashion style and video production skills have definitely evolved.,She began as a young girl with an eye for fashion and now she is a beauty and fashion guru for young girls everywhere. She was able to showcase her interests and fashion sense to her audience so effectively that they, too, started to emulate her interests.

## TIPS FOR BECOMING SUCCESSFUL ON YOUTUBE

If you want to become a beauty and fashion expert on YouTube like Bethany, here are some of the tips that she shared with aspiring YouTubers:

### 1. Authenticity is Key

Like Michelle Phan, Bethany also values authenticity above anything else. This is because she believes that being completely honest with how you portray yourself online is what actually attracts viewers and loyal fans.

### 2. Stay connected with your fans

Since fans are the foundation of any personality's fame, Bethany emphasizes the importance of staying connected and keeping in touch with them no matter how large. Make it a point to value your audience and appreciate their support. She told *AdWeek, "even if you just have five subscribers, you just have to focus on the audience you do have and create good content for them. As long as you're having fun with it, then that's all that matters."*

### 3. Have fun

Your goal should always involve having a good time regardless of whether you are conceptualizing, filming or editing your latest video. It will come across to your audience and your fans will enjoy your video more.

## 4. Do it with the right intentions

Bethany also underlines the importance of having the right intentions, especially when you are just starting out—"*Just watching a YouTube video, you don't really see how much work actually goes into it. It can be a five minute video, but that could take five days to work on. It's a big task, and it can feel like a chore if you go in with the intention of wanting to be successful,*" she told *AdWeek*.

## 5. Reply to their comments

When Bethany was just starting out as a YouTuber, she made sure to reply to her viewers' comments and feedback. At a young age, she knew that utilizing her network through different social media sites was very important in growing an audience and staying competitive in the virtual beauty and fashion community.

## 6. Encourage your fans to send you feedback

Bethany encourages her fans to send her photos of their finished products whenever they try a DIY project suggested by her. She tells her viewers to use a specific hashtag when posting a picture of a project that was inspired by some of her videos.

As you can see, turning a negative experience (such as cyberbullying for Bethany) into something positive could help you discover your passion or what you really want to do or achieve in life. She did not let her negative experience hinder her from staying positive and becoming such an inspiration to her fans.

# CHAPTER 6

# Technology YouTube

## Marques Brownlee

**YouTube Channel:** https://www.youtube.com/user/marquesbrownlee

**Videos Uploaded:** 727
**Views:** 234,267,181
**Subscribers:** 2,361,496

**Estimated Yearly Earnings: $40.8K - $653.2K**

**Vic Gundotra, the former VP of Social for Google, on his Google+ account called Marques, "the best technology reviewer on the planet right now."** But, unlike some of the YouTube personalities featured in this book, his popularity and success did not come to him as early and fast as the other YouTubers.

In fact, he only had 78 subscribers when he uploaded his 100th video. **After several years of staying active and**

**uploading quality content on YouTube, he now has 2.3 million subscribers and more than 200 million views.**

Marques Brownlee, a.k.a. MKBHD, is a 21-year-old full-time student and YouTube tech reviewer from New Jersey. **He told usatoday.com in an interview that his YouTube career started when he wanted to buy his first laptop computer when he was just a 14-year-old boy in high school.**

Marques researched and watched videos online to get an idea as to what laptop he wanted to buy. He saw helpful resources and was inspired to make his own video to discuss the points that he thought the other videos lacked. **The first ever video that he did was a hardware review in which he talked about the remote that came with the laptop that he purchased.**

After doing that, he decided to review software or programs through screencasting. Screencasting is basically recording your screen as you navigate through particular software on your computer.

His main goal was to help the people watching his videos with the process of their buying decision. He went about making a hundred videos by giving into the requests of the people watching and commenting on his videos.

It wasn't until he uploaded a tutorial on how to install Safari on a Windows computer that he realized his influence on YouTube. **He uploaded the video, went to bed and**

**was surprised to find out the next day that his video received around 7,000 views.**

*"...it was the first time that I could see that people really cared about these time sensitive stuff, and people actually cared about the videos that I could make."*

After making hundreds of tutorials or reviews of free software, a company whose products are paid software finally reached out to Marques. They gave him the license to give a tutorial, review or practically do whatever he wanted with their product. Then another company approached him and gave him a keyboard to review.

Back then, Marques didn't think that people were actually into reviewing hardware; he did not even have a camera to make hardware tech reviews. He only had the web cam on his laptop.

After some time, more and more companies reached out to him to have their products reviewed. He also buys some of the gadgets that he wants to feature on his channel. Since the rise of his channel's popularity and credibility, Marques gets his hands on a lot of different gadgets or tech stuff before they even hit the market.

**The YouTube success story of Marques is a great testament of what passion, perseverance, patience, and hard work could do for your YouTube career.** He started off as a young teenage boy who did hundreds of screen casts of free software and emerged more or less seven years later as the 21- year-old who built an empire out of making consumer electronics themed YouTube videos. To date, his main channel, MKBHD, boasts more than two million subscribers and his video views are over two hundred million in total.

## TIPS FROM MKBHD HIMSELF

Marques uploaded a series of videos on his channel in which he talked about some strategies for starting your own YouTube channel from ground zero. If you're looking into starting your own channel about technology, you might want to consider tips from the Go-to guy in technology himself, MKBHD:

### 1. Select a Tech Video Type

A channel about technology could either be about software, hardware, tech news, or a combination of the three. MKBHD suggests that the easiest type of tech to start reviewing is software.

It is the easiest because anyone could make a video demonstrating how a certain type of software is used or how it can be maximized at no cost.

**Marques actually started his YouTube career by using a free downloadable software called CamStudio** that basically records the activity on your computer screen. He used this to film a lot of his demos or reviews of other free software products that he got his hands on.

You could also talk about tech news on your channel, but this is more challenging and competitive. First and foremost, tech news is much more difficult to provide because it is time sensitive. You really have to be on top of the latest product developments, rumors, or discoveries for you to be able to come up with current and valuable information.

Secondly, tech news has become saturated and the competition has definitely become tougher. You have to be able to come up with something unique or different in order to stand out.

The third type of tech video that you could focus on is hardware. When you choose to make hardware tutorials or demos, you have to have decent recording equipment and, of course, basic video editing skills.

You also have to get gadgets or up-to-date tech to review. You can either buy them yourself or seek and negotiate for sponsorship deals.

## 2. Establish your brand

On YouTube, it's not only important to focus on creating good quality content for your videos, you also have to appeal to your audience by establishing your brand through your channel design, logo, intro/outro, and overall branding. MKBHD emphasized the importance of having a consistent color scheme or graphics on your channel for you to be easily identified by YouTube viewers.

## 3. Use Appropriate Equipment

Of course, it would be impossible to make a high quality video without the proper equipment. You have to at least have a reliable camera and a microphone, especially if you want to make tech reviews of hardware products.

MKBHD takes his craft very seriously. He spends a lot of his time after school working on his YouTube videos. He is very meticulous when it comes to making his videos from start to finish. Whenever he thinks about the topic or technology that he wants to feature next, he considers what he would want to watch and plans his productions accordingly.

He exerts a lot of effort to meet the standards that he sets for his videos; he stays on top of everything from the video style to how he wants to discuss the topic, what content he wants to see in his description box, and especially the kind of language that he uses in his reviews.

One of the most common challenges that Marques experiences when he makes his videos is the technicality or level of diffi- culty of his language. He wants to be able to cater to both the experts and amateurs in the tech world. He wants people who know a lot more than he does to find some useful information from his channel, but he also wants those who are just getting into tech to easily understand what he is talking about—***"I definitely think a lot about the intersection of these two groups and what kind of language could be used to talk to both groups of people."***

He also noticed that a lot of the other tech blogs or channels prefer to be as objective as possible when it comes to reviewing products. They only tend to narrate the facts about the prod- ucts and not really give their opinion of them.

On the other hand, Marques makes sure that he gives his honest opinion about the products, to give his viewers an idea about the product that they are interested in acquiring. His expert and honest opinion together with his high quality videos have made MKBHD one of the best YouTube tech reviewers that ever existed.

# CHAPTER 7

# Powerful How-To Stars

YouTube can make everything fun and interesting for anyone, even learning. It has become the multi-billion dollar video sharing platform that we know and love today because of the variety of content that it offers.

It has everything from comedy and gaming to music, food, lifestyle, and any form of entertainment that you could possibly want. It also has a lot of educational channels that foster learning and skill development.

Some of the most popular content that is generated by YouTubers usually **involves them producing How-to videos, tutorials, or a full ten to fifteen minute video of them extensively talking about a particular topic.** One of the most popular YouTube personalities who is fond of sharing his knowledge and research on a concept is the man behind Vsauce, Michael Stevens.

## Vsauce

**YouTube Channel:** https://www.youtube.com/user/
Vsauce Videos Uploaded: 309

**Views:** 776,515,149
**Subscribers:** 8,595,020

**Estimated Yearly Earnings: $55.9K - $895.1K**

Vsauce is a YouTube channel founded by Michael Stevens, a double degree holder (neuropsychology and English literature) with a curious mind and a passion for learning and explaining things.

**His channel has captured the attention of millions of people due to its interesting, factual, and educational content.** Vsauce is basically a channel that investigates and explains the science, mathematics, and even history behind anything and everything under the sun.

With over 700 million views and eight million subscribers, **Michael Stevens is one of the most popular and successful educators on YouTube.** Michael is an American living in the UK. He joined YouTube in 2007 but it wasn't until 2010 that he launched his main channel. Growing up, Michael has always loved being curious and learning about everything, even the most mundane things.

At a young age, he noticed that he often talked to himself out loud. He found that when he talked and explained things to himself out loud, even if no one was around, he was able to understand and appreciate simple and complex thoughts, ideas, or concepts.

It was during high school when he discovered his passion for learning and explaining things. **They were required to deliver an informative speech and talk about any topic that they wanted.** He decided to give an eight-minute speech about *ketchup*—its history, etymology, significance to society, viscosity, and other interesting facts about it. He won a medal because of that speech and from then on he knew what he was good at and what he loved doing.

## HOW VSAUCE STARTED

During the early days of YouTube, back in 2006-2007, Michael watched a video on YouTube entitled "The Shining", which is basically a horror movie that was re-cut to look like a trailer for a feel good, romantic comedy film. Back then, only a skilled editor or a production team would be able to produce such material, but the recut version of The Shining was actually done by a single person. Michael was amazed by how one person could twist a story and transform it into something completely different, so he wanted to try it for himself.

*"...Shining was made by one guy, for one competition, and he warped the entire movie, and to have that kind of power, I thought 'I gotta do this, I've got to learn how to edit,' and the first projects that I made were literally copies of that format."*

He made his own version by warping the comedy movie "Ferris Bueller's Day Off" to make it look like a horror film. His video caught the attention of Jeff Rubin from CollegeHumor and it greatly encouraged him to make more videos. It was during the election period that he decided to make politics the central theme of his episodes.

Not long after, he was discovered by Ben Relles, the creator of a comedy network called Barely Political where he worked as a cameraman. When Barely Political started making The Key of Awesome, which features parodies of famous songs, Michael thought that he wasn't "musical" so he thought of making a video game themed channel instead.

## THE ORIGIN OF THE NAME VSAUCE

You'll be surprised that the term "Vsauce" actually meant nothing back then. Michael used a random name generator and—voilà—"Vsauce" popped up. It initially meant nothing but it eventually evolved into a channel that features Michael talking about the things that mean a great deal to him. *(source: Meet Vsauce –Sixty Symbols published on youtube.com)*

He draws the attention of his YouTube viewers by discussing and asking questions that range from the most ordinary to the wildest, and out of the box topics. He comes up with the material that he wants to feature in his next video by thinking of the concepts that could be strung together to form a common theme. He then comes up with a catchy title to get a viewer to click on his videos out of curiosity. The titles of his videos are somewhere along the lines of **"Is Your Red Same as My Red?" "What Color is A Mirror?" or "Why Are Things Creepy?"**

When he works on an episode for Vsauce, he comprehensively researches everything about the topic he or his viewers are interested in. It takes him about five to seven days to research and write about a certain topic. While he is doing his research, he casually shares his ideas with other people to see how they would respond. This allows him to verify if he is going in the right direction.

He takes his time in doing research because he really wants to master the material that he is working on. In fact, the information that he shares in each episode is only a small part of what he really learned and researched. Whenever he works on a new episode, he makes sure that he overly learns the topic for him to confidently say to himself that he is sufficiently familiar with the topic.

This is because he wants to prepare himself well in case a person comes up to him with a follow up question or requests clarification about the topics he has discussed.

## TIPS ON HOW TO RESEARCH LIKE MICHAEL

In a video uploaded by Sixty Symbols on YouTube, Michael shared the step-by-step process of how he does research for a particular topic for his videos.

**1.** To get things started, Michael goes on to Wikipedia to read the most updated information about his topic of interest. He finds Wikipedia a good source to check whether certain information is still up to date.

**2.** He then reads a lot of academic research papers about the same topic to broaden his awareness and knowledge of the topic.

**3.** He also watches a lot of videos and lectures about the topic. He then cites the sources that he used for a particular video in the description box when he eventually finishes and uploads an episode. The great thing about this technique is that it also allows him to connect with the people that he used as references.

**4.** To make sure that he doesn't share faulty or inaccurate information, he consults his friends or connects with people who are experts in the field.

## MARKETING LESSONS FROM MICHAEL'S 2013 TED TALK

*"The trick in education, is to teach in such a way that people only find out they're learning when it's too late."*

### 1. "People love a good explanation"

Michael pointed out the fact that everyone enjoys and appreciates a good explanation, even if at first he doesn't find the topic interesting. Michael's ability to generate enthusiasm by thinking of the best title that would get a viewer to click on a video and eventually subscribe has definitely helped with his channel's success.

### 2. "If you look closely enough, and you take the time, anything can be interesting to anyone because everything is related in some way to something they care about"

The great thing about his videos is that you come and watch his videos to learn one thing, but you end up knowing more besides. He generates a lot of his ideas from his viewers' suggestions. He also entertains silly questions such as "How much does a fart weigh?" then he does his research and answers the question seriously. He then uses this opportunity to spark their curiosity and they not only know the answer to their question but they also learn more about other concepts related to it.

### 3. "I've noticed that the most operative motive behind someone sharing one of my videos—promoting them via word-of-mouth —isn't so much about me as it is about them"

Michael noticed that there is a higher chance of someone sharing his videos when they can relate to the topic to some extent, or if the content of his videos somehow reflects back to them— *"so I've found that one of the best ways to gain attentive listeners is not be who you think your audience wants you to be, but instead say and make and show things that allow your audience to be who they want to be."*

# CHAPTER 8

# Marketing Strategies for up-and-coming YouTubers

If you want to make easy money through YouTube, you might want to think again. One of the things that you should remember is that, for a YouTuber to generate a significant amount of income for his channel, he must be able to gain a substantial amount of views and subscribers.

As you have read in the profiles of the YouTube millionaires featured in the previous chapters, YouTube fame cannot be attained overnight. It usually takes a lot of trial and error, research, and time in the production and filming of a video before a new YouTube user can reach a thousand views, or a hundred subscribers.

Take, for example, the story of Marques Brownlee from MKBHD; despite uploading 100 videos, he only had 78 subscribers.

There is no secret formula to attain YouTube success. Few YouTube millionaires ever thought that they would one day have millions and even billions of people watching their videos.

In fact, no one can predict and be one hundred percent certain about what or who the next big thing, hit, or trend will be. But **one way to make sure that you are going in the right direction towards being YouTube famous is by starting today.**

Many of the most successful self-made YouTubers did not have a specific category in mind when they were just starting to build their channel. For instance, Michael Stevens from Vsauce initially created his channel for video gaming, not for science and education.

The point is that you don't necessarily have to have a successful niche, especially when you are new to creating original content and editing videos. Like Rosanna Pansino from Nerdy Nummies, you could first experiment with the type of content that you and your viewers would like most.

Once you've determined the content that best fits your personality and preference of your audience, **work your way up and be consistent in producing high quality content.** But to give you an idea as to what kind of content your channel could focus on, here is a list of categories of YouTube's Google Preferred Channels according to tubefilter.com:

- Anime & Teen Animation Video Gaming
- Music
- Family & Children's Interest Beauty

- Trucks, & Racing
- Food & Recipes
- Cars
- Weightlifting, Workouts, & Wellness News
- Science & Education
- Sports
- Comedy Entertainment & Pop Culture Technology

## WAYS TO GROW YOUR YOUTUBE VIEWS AND SUBSCRIBERS

If you can recall the story of why Lancôme made Michelle Phan their spokesperson in the online world, you'll remember that, despite spending a lot of money on making a high quality video with top make-up artists and models, not a lot of people were watching their videos.

Even if you have set-up an awesome channel and have created videos with great content, they will seem irrelevant if only a handful of people watch them.

Once you already have your YouTube channels set up and have determined the kind of content that you want to focus on, you can learn strategies on how you can grow your channel and make a considerable income from it.

## A. TIPS TO GET MORE SUBSCRIBERS

When you are able to successfully create a YouTube profile and upload videos, having your first subscribers will always be exciting, especially when they are from outside your circle. But how can you attract more? Gaining subscribers on YouTube is simple, but not easy. You have to learn and apply strategies to be able to have new subscribers daily. Here are some suggestions on how you can do it:

## 1. Respond and Interact with your present fanbase

One of the most effective ways to attract more subscribers is by interacting with your present audience. When you relate or share interesting conversations with your existing audience, your channel, especially the comments section of your videos, will be filled with a community of YouTube users who exchange useful information with one another. This will encourage a YouTube user who visits your channel for the first time to subscribe because your channel (not only has videos with useful content, but it also has a community of active YouTube users who share educated conversations.)

## 2. Be creative with your titles

Do not underestimate the power of a great title. It is important to compose your title with as many keywords that people usually search for. A YouTube user is more likely to type in a general subject than a specific one, so make sure that you choose the words in your title wisely to make it more searchable.

## 3. Prompt your viewers to subscribe

Another way to generate more subscribers is to put a reminder on each of your videos to click the subscribe button on your channel. Use a call to action to really encourage a viewer to subscribe if he or she comes across one of your videos. The most commonly used examples of call to actions by famous

YouTubers include: "Please subscribe to my channel," "To watch more videos, click here," or "Share this video."

You could format your call to action by using annotations, end cards, or by talking to the viewers directly through your video.

## 4. Continuously and Consistently upload videos

Ryan Higa is one of the few YouTubers with the longest running YouTube channels. He has witnessed how successful YouTubers gradually lose their presence when they stop uploading new videos for some period of time. If a YouTube user visits your channel and sees that you only have one video upload, he might not be interested in subscribing. The bottom line is that more and more people will be enthused to press the subscribe button when you frequently upload interesting and quality videos.

## 5. Maximize the use of YouTube's Fan Finder Program

YouTube created Fan Finder to help YouTubers promote their channel. Fan Finder is basically a program wherein YouTubers can submit snippets of their videos for it to be advertised as pre-roll ads on other YouTube videos. Any YouTuber can apply and submit their videos to the program. When they are accepted, their video clips will be displayed through different videos, free of charge!

# B. TIPS TO GET MORE VIEWS

## 1. Base your videos on trending topics

It is a good idea every now and then for the theme of your videos to revolve around trending topics. This will allow you to gain a lot more attention from other YouTube users because your channel is up-to-date and relevant. More people will also see your channel because your videos contain popular tags and trends.

## 2. Collaborate with other YouTubers

Boyce Avenue significantly widened their reach when they started collaborating with other YouTubers. They frequently do covers with different artists when they upload a new video.

In fact, the majority of the famous YouTubers such as Ryan Higa, Rosanna Pansino, Jenna Marbles, and The Fine Bros. have formed deep friendships with their fellow YouTubers because of their collaboration. A lot of the famous YouTube personalities perceive one another as members of a community that aims to educate, inform or entertain people, which is why they work together to build one another's brands instead of competing with each other.

## 3. Use Proper Tags and Keywords

A lot of up-and-coming YouTubers overlook the importance of using tags and keywords. It will greatly help your channel gain attention if you not only think of the phrases that you put in your title, but also the keywords and tags that you type in your video's description. You can use keywords such as the format and style of your new upload. You can describe it as a rant, parody, spoof, or review.

## 4. Make sure your thumbnails spark interest

Besides optimizing your title, keywords, or tags, you can also make use of engaging thumbnails. Make sure that your videos look appealing to attract clicks, generate views, and subscribers.

## C. PROMOTE YOUR CHANNEL ON OTHER SOCIAL MEDIA PLATFORMS

One of the best ways to promote your channel and videos is none other than cross promoting your YouTube channel on your other social media accounts. Here are some practical tips on how to use platforms such as Facebook, Twitter, and forums to generate more views, subscribers, and, eventually, income!

### 1. Facebook

As you probably know, Facebook has become the most popular social media network today. It is also one of the easiest ways to promote, advertise or market your brand or products. Here are some simple ways to promote your YouTube handle on Facebook:

- Create a Fan Page for your YouTube channel
- Invite your Facebook friends to like your Fan Page
- Share your YouTube videos on your page
- Establish your presence and be personal
- Share content or posts other than your YouTube channel or video Monitor your Facebook Fan page's analytics

### 2. Twitter

Twitter has become one of the most used microblogging websites ever. Celebrities, atheletes, YouTube personalities and billions of people use this great social platform to share their thoughts, interests or practically any trending issue or topic.

Here are some tips on how to use Twitter to promote your YouTube channel:

- Encourage your followers to retweet (RT) the links that you share
- Use better hashtags
- Engage with your followers through Twitter Chats
- Host Twitter Contests about your YouTube channel

### 3. Forums

Another way to promote your channel on other platforms is by joining forums. Forums are essentially comprised of intelligent online discussions about relevant topics. Joining forums could help you get in touch with experts, or people with the same interests as you. One of the forums most commonly used by YouTubers is reddit.com.

## FINAL TIPS TO KEEP IN MIND

If you are an aspiring YouTuber, consider these tips to help you successfully launch your channel and hopefully grow your views and subscribers:

### 1. Never Spam

The last thing that you should do is bombard your potential audience with repetitive and annoying promotional tactics just to get them to visit your channel or watch your videos. Instead of focusing on promoting your channel by commenting on every viral or trending video that you see or sending them hourly emails, focus on improving your material and the content of your videos.

## 2. Take copyright and plagiarism seriously

If you don't want your channel to be suspended or taken down, you have to be very careful with what you publish. Focus on your ideas, and make original content.

## 3. Perseverance is key

When you are just starting to build your channel, it is important to push through and not give up easily, especially if you really want to have a successful YouTube channel. Marques Brownlee never would have attained such incredible success if he stopped with his 100th video with only 78 subscribers. As I said at the beginning of this book, turning to YouTube to earn easy money is not an option, primarily because **building a channel is far from easy; it takes a lot of time, patience and practice before you capture your successful niche.**

# CHAPTER 9

# Viral Videos and Success Tweaks

On May 28, 2015 in celebration of YouTube's 10th year anniversary, YouTube Spotlight published The A-Z of YouTube: Celebrating 10 Years. The clip featured the best of the best viral videos and trends in the past decade. As expected, just after **three days since it was published, the 10-year anniversary video with the hashtag #HappyBirthdayYouTube was already streamed 8.9 million times.**

The short clip contained 75 references of the most memorable YouTube dance craze, personalities, and characters from Grumpy Cat, Harlem Shake to Felix Baumgartner's Stratos jump for Red Bull. **To date, the Red Bull Stratos jump still holds the title for the most viewed live stream on YouTube.**

But, the real question is, how did these videos become viral?

Or as a YouTuber or marketer, how could you make the people who view your videos click on the share button?

If you're on YouTube, you're probably wondering as to how these videos made the list out of the millions, if not billions of other YouTubers and videos. With millions of content that is uploaded on YouTube everyday, its very challenging, especially for up and coming YouTubers or start-up brands to make their presence known or at least, get their message across online. This is the main reason why marketers as well as all the other YouTubers need to think differently.

**Kevin Allocca, the Trends Manager of YouTube, discussed three factors that make videos go viral on his** 2012 TED Talk:

- **Tastemakers**
  He explained the role of tastemakers by using the example of Yosemitebear Mountain Double Rainbow, which now has 41.6M views. The creator of the video did not intend his video to go viral; he just genuinely wanted to share his incredible, and probably once in a lifetime experience in witnessing a full double rainbow.

  Allocca explained that the video originally did not have that much attention until Jimmy Kimmel tweeted about it. ***Tastemakers* are basically the people, like Kimmel, who start trends and introduce the interesting content to a wider and larger community.**

- **Participation**
  He then explained participation through the case of Rebecca Black's single, Friday. It suddenly became one of the most viral and most viewed videos on the year of its release when blogs started writing articles about it.

With such a very strong reaction from the audience that have read the blogs and watched the video, more and more people, especially YouTubers referenced to it, and even made parodies of it. The fact that people actually took the time and exerted effort in making their own version of the song/music video is **proof that people are not just entertained by the videos they find online, but they are also willing to engage and *participate*.**

▪ **Unexpectedness**

Another key factor of viral videos according to Allocca is unexpectedness. He used the illustration of the video about a protesting cyclist named Casey Neistat. Instead of ranting about his issues on road policies for bicycles like what traditional protesters would do, he made a video about his actual experience of getting a ticket for not biking in the proper lane.

**He took a rather radical and unexpected approach to address his complaint.** He filmed himself again riding his bike *without ever leaving the bike lane* (as instructed by the officer who gave him the ticket) despite the road works and other obstructions that were along the said lane.

As a result, he ended up falling from his bike multiple times, bumping into a cab, or getting himself into a delivery truck because he *never* left the bike lane. Fortunately, he was able to get his message across in a peaceful but effective way. His video now has more than 14M views.

Any online video creator or marketer always wants the most exposure for their videos to generate views and of course, get their target audience engaged. Although, there's no secret formula to making a viral video, you can still do a lot to create video content that would make the viewers watch it again, or better yet, share it on social media.

If you're an online business start-up entrepreneur who wants to market his products or services through videos, or an up and coming YouTuber who wants to increase his ratings and number of views or subscribers, then I suggest that you try out some of the strategies listed below:

## 1. Get Their Attention Right Away

If you are thinking of making a video with a long intro, think again. One major element of viral videos is that they are able to **capture the attention of their viewers swiftly.** The first five to sevens seconds of your video is crucial in order to make the viewer stay and watch the whole thing. The bottom line is that the first few seconds of your video should be enticing enough to make your viewer and potential subscriber or client interested. This means you might reconsider putting your logos or product shots at the very beginning of your videos.

## 2. Ask for Likes

A common misconception among budding YouTubers is that they assume that having a very high number of subscribers would ensure that their videos would get enough reach and even go viral. Although a lot of subscribers would indeed help with getting views right away, it is not a really good predictor of it going viral. **A more effective approach would be asking other YouTube users to 'like' the video that you have just uploaded**. Doing so would make your video appear to the feeds of the people subscribed to those channels. The goal is to engage with other YouTube channels with similar niche and approach as yours.

## 3. Share It on Blogs and Sites

Karen Cheng, the girl behind the viral video Girl Learns to Dance in a Year (TIME LAPSE) shared tips on how to make videos go viral. She explained how she really worked hard to make her video appear on the front page of YouTube. After publishing her video, she posted it on her Twitter and Facebook accounts.

She also took the time to submit it to other websites and blogs such as Hacker News and Reddit. On day one, she was able to gain 80,000 views. The next day, because of ranking first on the GetMotivated subreddit, other sites such as Mashable and Huffington Post also wrote an article about it.

By sharing her story on Reddit and attracting the interest of other blogs, her video had 800,000 views on day two. Just after three days of uploading her video, with a lot of traffic from blogs who wrote articles about it, it gained 1.8M views and it made YouTube's front page. You can do this when you upload a new video by notifying small bloggers and partnering with them.

## 3. Find the Balance Between Surprising and Shocking

During the initial phases of creating video content, think about a concept or a theme that would most likely evoke strong emotions or reactions from your audience. However, you should really be cautious when it comes to finding the balance between both reactions because it affects the amount of shares of the video. One of the most popular goals of online video creators is to make their viewers laugh out loud or feel inspired and motivated to take action or do something different.

## 4. Being Viral isn't just having Millions of Views

The primary goal of all video creators is to generate as much views as they can. However, going viral should not only be their only goal. Being able to establish a larger following or translating views into sales (for brands) is also as important. This is why as a video creator, you should be able to re-think your objectives as to why you want your videos to go viral in the first place. This will help you focus on creating a more effective content and marketing strategy because you have successfully established your goals.

## 5. Check Your Title for Revisions

Karen Cheng, the creator of *Girl Learns to Dance in a Year (TIME LAPSE)*, suggested that other YouTube content creators should learn how to write a viral title. She even gave examples of bad to best title choices:

- Bad- *My Journey of Dance, a Year of Moment*
- Better- *I learned to Dance in a Year*
- Even Better- *Girl Learns to Dance in a Year*
- Best- *Girl Learns to Dance in a Year (TIME LAPSE)*

Having the right title is essential for your video to get as many hits and tags as possible whenever a potential viewer types in a keyword on the search box. To guide you in thinking of the best title for your video Chen suggests to fill in the blank to this sentence: *"Hey did you see the video of_____ "* whatever you put in that line, that's your title.

As you could see, you could still do a lot of last minute touches to increase the probability of your video in going viral. According to a study conducted at Elon University, there are actually nine characteristics that make up videos that go viral.

These are the title length, laughter, run time, element of surprise, music quality, talent, youth presence, and element of irony. With enough patience, perseverance, and experience, you are well on your way to finding your niche, having a breakthrough, and hopefully someday get your videos and channel on YouTube's front page!!

# Conclusion

Now that you have read some of the success stories of the famous YouTubers from different genres, I hope that you are **inspired to follow in their footsteps and start working on building your YouTube channel today.**

I trust that you have gained a deeper understanding of the different ways in which you could maximize your YouTube channel to earn money.

Having millions of views and subscribers might seem like a long shot, especially when you are just starting your channel. But with the lessons that you have learned in this book and the success stories that you have read, I can confidently say that you are starting on the right track to becoming the next You-Tube millionaire!

I wish you luck in your endeavors!

**Check it out: Blow up your YouTube Channel today connecting with me and how I might be able to help you!**

Video Blog, Articles and Services:

- www.velocityvideosonline.com

You can also reach me at:

- **Specialreport:** http://speakupmore.com
- **Twitter:** https://twitter.com/velocityVid
- **Facebook:** http://www.facebook.com/ mrseankmichael

Thank you and have a most excellent day!